Landmarks

Landmarks

Nathanael O'Reilly

Copyright Nathanael O'Reilly 2024
All rights reserved

ISBN:978-1-962148-02-3
LOC: 2023952546

Cover Photo: Nathanael O'Reilly

Lamar University Literary Press
Beaumont, TX

Gratitude

Thanks always to Tricia, my partner for twenty-five years, and our daughter Celeste, and to my parents Paul and Moira O'Reilly. Big thanks to the following people for friendship, support, opportunities and inspiration: Sean Scarisbrick, Lachlan Brown, rob mclennan, Alex Lemon, Damien B. Donnelly, Annemarie Ní Churreáin, Jessica Traynor, Matt Hohner, Anne Casey, Mark Roberts, Cedrick May, Penny Ingram, Jeremy Bennett, Heather Horner, Aisling Keogh and Mari Maxwell.

Recent Poetry from Lamar University Literary Press

Lisa Adams, *Xuai*
Walter Bargen, *My Other Mother's Red Mercedes*
David Bowles, *Liminal*
Jerry Bradley, *Collapsing into Possibility*
Mark Busby, *Through Our Times*
Julie Chappell, *Mad Habits of a Life*
Stan Crawford, *Resisting Gravity*
Glover Davis, *My Cap of Darkness*
William Virgil Davis, *The Bones Poems*
Jeffrey DeLotto, *Voices Writ in Sand*
Chris Ellery, *Elder Tree*
Dede Fox, *On Wings of Silence*
Alan Gann, *That's Entertainment*
Larry Griffin, *Cedar Plums*
Michelle Hartman, *Irony and Irrelevance*
Michael Jennings, *Crossings: A Record of Travel*
Gretchen Johnson, *A Trip Through Downer, Minnesota*
Betsy Joseph, *Only So Many Autumns*
Ulf Kirchdorfer, *Chewing Green Leaves*
Jim McGarrah, *A Balancing Act*
J. Pittman McGehee, *Nod of Knowing*
Laurence Musgrove, *Bluebonnet Sutras*
Benjamin Myers, *The Family Book of Martyrs*
Janice Northerns, *Some Electric Hum*
Godspower Oboido, *Wandering Feet on Pebbled Shores*
Carol Coffee Reposa, *Underground Musicians*
Jan Seale, *The Parkinson Poems*
Steven Schroeder, *the moon, not the finger, pointing*
Glen Sorestad, *Hazards of Eden*
Vincent Spina, *The Sumptuous Hills of Gulfport*
W.K. Stratton, *Betrayal Creek*
Wally Swist, *Invocation*
Ken Waldman, *Sports Page*
Loretta Diane Walker, *Ode to My Mother's Voice*
Dan Williams, *Past Purgatory, a Distant Paradise*
Jonas Zdanys, *The Angled Road*

For information on these and other Lamar University Literary Press books go to www.Lamar.edu/literarypress

Acknowledgements

I am grateful to the editors of the following publications in which many of these poems first appeared:

Verity La
Mascara Literary Review
Adelaide Literary Magazine
Rochford Street Review
A New Ulster
The Elevation Review
Trasna
Loch Raven Review
Dusie
Meniscus
Social Alternatives
Olney Magazine
Headstuff
The Dan Poets Anthology
The Antonym
Pendemic
Bluepepper
FourXFour
Tincture
Writing Texas, Volume 9
Anthropocene
Westerly
Strukturriss
Red Weather
Neologism Poetry Journal
Melbourne Culture Corner
Prosopisia: An International Journal of Poetry and Creative Writing
Live Encounters Poetry & Writing
Literati Magazine
Eclectica Magazine
Identity Theory
New World Writing Quarterly
No News: 90 Poets Reflect on a Unique BBC Newscast
Glasgow Review of Books
fourW thirty-one NEW WRITING
Poetry d'Amour Anthology 2023

Kalliope X
In Parentheses: New Modernism
The Wexford Bohemian
Ponder Review
The Stony Thursday Book
An Aítiúil: An Anthology
Wellington Street Review
Crow of Minerva
Adelaide Literary Awards Anthology 2020

CONTENTS

13	I. Prelude
14	Homeland
19	II. Overture
20	How to Fall Out of a Pine Tree
22	From Ballarat to Brisbane
24	Tingalpa
25	Fortitude
27	Volume
28	Port Fairy
30	Michael Quigley
32	Scarification
33	Ritual
35	III. Movement
36	Freight Train
37	Inbetween Days
40	Chords & Lyrics
41	Elsewhere
42	February
43	International Arrivals
45	Sketchbook
47	Asylum
48	Virus as Metaphor
50	Profit
51	Bookpeople
52	Trail Ride
53	Holy Ghost
54	Mountain Forest Campground
55	WWJD?
56	Komatsu
57	The Suburb of the Future
58	Duck Feast
59	White Privilege
61	Adjustment
62	Preparations for the Fourth

63	External Composition
64	Acorns
65	Reprieve
66	Lake Effects
67	Campus Events
68	Rainwater
69	Lego Building
70	Protection/Prevention
71	Notes & Feedback
72	Summer Rain
73	Departed
75	IV. Middle Eight
76	Manifestations
77	A Prayer to Nick Cave
78	Good Friday, 1930
79	Warhol
80	Wheat Work
81	Sweet Movement
82	Preparation
83	Lodestars
85	V. Interlude
86	Homecoming
87	Townland
89	Pilgrimage
90	July Evening
91	Field Work
92	Sanctuary
93	VI. Crescendo
94	Confession
95	Safe Home
96	Marching
97	Dark Angel
98	Florentine Discourse
99	Santa Maria Maggiore
100	Homesickness (Remix)
103	Playa Tortugas

105	VII. Coda

106	Crossings
107	After the Pandemic
109	Homescape

111	Notes

113	Bio

I.
PRELUDE

Homeland

I left my homeland like a magpie
searching for attractive objects

I left my homeland and travelled
to another hemisphere

I left my homeland like my ancestors
carrying my possessions in both hands

I left in the middle of winter

I left my homeland
breaking my mother's heart

I left in pursuit of love and adventure

I left trying to escape the ordinary
rejecting expectations and norms

I left intending to return

I left after selling my skateboard
and giving my car to my brother

I left after boxing my books and letters
storing them in my parents' garage

I left my homeland when my sisters
were twelve and seven, made it difficult
for them to truly know me

I left ten days before my father turned forty-five

I left in an excited state, full of dreams, plans and fantasies

I left innocent, naïve, unaware of the consequences

I left my homeland, abandoned
family, friends, people I loved

I left my homeland following family
tradition, crossing oceans like my Irish
English, Welsh and Portuguese ancestors

I left thinking I was brave, independent
resourceful, adventurous, admirable
I left believing I was leaving behind
a future with limited opportunities

I left thinking people who stayed home
were parochial, sheltered, timid

I left my homeland failing to understand
I would lose part of myself, my identity

I left eucalyptus, molasses, brown rivers
filled with sandbars and snags, white sand
beaches, salt spray, rockpools, headlands
cliffs, caves, seaweed, bush, mountains
wheat fields, dairy farms, sheep stations
shearing sheds, haystacks, electric fences
milking sheds, bitumen basketball courts
cricket fields, footy ovals, irrigation channels
grain silos, country pubs, colonial architecture
front verandahs, corrugated iron roofs, lighthouses
breaking surf, ancestors resting in cemeteries
weatherboard houses, Hills Hoists, backyard
vegie patches, brick barbecues, galahs
cockatoos, kangaroos, koalas and trams

I left unconsciously breaking bonds
ending relationships, eliminating futures
hurting loved ones, insulting people
who cared for me and wanted me to stay

I left like a sheep jumping a barbed-wire fence

I left like a receding tide
I left like a season ending
I left like the sun setting
I left like the sun rising

I left my homeland, hurtled through space
escaped gravity, entered a new orbit

I left after two years of working
planning, saving and self-denial
living on bread, pasta and porridge

I left taking chances, embracing
the unknown, putting faith in the unseen

I left carrying a black suitcase
packed with hand-written journals
notebooks, letters, poems and photographs

I left late last century, twelve days
after my twenty-second birthday

I left to the sound of The Cure
U2, REM, Van Morrison
The Smiths, Counting Crows, Crowded House

I left wearing faded blue corduroy
jeans, a burgundy windcheater
and scuffed brown Blundstones

I left wearing a silver earring
fringe hanging over my left eye
vintage ring on my right hand
leather bracelet on my left wrist

I left believing I was in love

I left selfishly

I left my homeland, missed twenty-firsts
engagement parties, weddings, births
anniversaries, funerals, family reunions

I left my homeland, missed embraces
kisses, handshakes, affection, love
I left alone

I left temporarily
accidentally became a permanent exile
made decision after decision
that made it harder and harder to return

II.
OVERTURE

How to Fall Out of a Pine Tree

select the tallest tree
in the backyard and reach

up with both hands
grasp the lowest branch

place your right foot against
the trunk at waist-height

support your weight
with both hands and swing

your left foot
onto the trunk

walk your feet up to the lowest
branch then pull yourself

into a sitting position
pause   rest and breathe

lift your feet from beneath
one by one onto the branch

then stand while grasping
the trunk   pause   reach up

for the branch above your head
and repeat the previous actions

until you ascend to the highest
branch that supports your weight

sit and gaze over corrugated rooftops
look down into neighbour's yards

spy on garden sheds, vegie patches
Hills Hoists, compost bins and swing sets

let go of the branch and balance
marvel at your poise and skill

fall backwards through needles
and branches towards earth

land on the lowest branch
grasp firmly and slow your heart

look around for witnesses
gently lower yourself to earth

walk towards the back door
upon trembling bloody legs

From Ballarat to Brisbane

After Joe Brainard

I remember falling out of a pine tree
at 2 Waller Avenue in Ballarat

I remember my eyes puffing up
after playing in waist-high grass
on the vacant block down the street
and the pretty nurse sticking
a needle in my bum at the hospital

I remember riding a black horse
sixteen hands high while wearing red
gumboots and red corduroy jeans

I remember burning my tongue
with tomato soup at recess
in the shelter shed
at Redan Primary School

I remember the neighbour's German Shepherd
nipping at my arse when I scaled the fence
after retrieving a tennis ball from their backyard

I remember riding my red bike
into a puddle beside Lake Wendouree
sinking in mud up to my handlebars

I remember carving my initials
into a branch high up inside
the eucalyptus tree with a pocketknife

I remember breaking my mate's thumb
while taking a mark playing footy
on the oval at lunchtime in grade one

I remember standing in the dirt driveway
of 50 Larbonya Crescent, Capalaba
on New Year's Day thinking *It's 1980!*

I remember my mate Ian finding a wallet
stuffed with eight fifty-dollar notes
at the shopping centre and buying
a dozen cinnamon doughnuts

I remember playing barefoot
lunchtime rugby and red rover
ripping uniforms and skinning knees

I remember the headmaster
summoning me to his office
giving me six of the best
for playing outside in the rain

I remember moving from Ballarat to Brisbane
when I was six—leaving behind my mates
and everything I'd ever known

Tingalpa

The bush spread to the reservoir's
edge. Water stretched out of sight
around the peninsula. Wind-blown
waves chopped across to the distant
shore. Kids searched the waterline
for skimming stones, sent them skipping
into the distance as galahs squawked
in the gums and shat from on high.
Snakes bellied through undergrowth,
redbacks wove webs between boughs
and magpies swooped passing bikes.
Flies settled in colonies on uniforms,
crawled inside nostrils on sweltering
afternoons after long state school days.

Fortitude

We rode our bikes to school along Parkside
Drive, Balaclava Road and Graham Street,
dodging swooping magpies, and out of town
to Mooroopna, Lemnos and Congupna
across rivers through bushland and orchards
of ripe apricots, peaches and pears.

We spent blistering summers at the pool
competing to hold our breath, bellyflop
from the diving board, backflip off the blocks,
swim the length underwater on one breath,
tried to impress bored brown glistening girls.

Our mob skated down Wyndham Street, wheels
clicking on the cracks between concrete slabs,
at the War Memorial, at North Tech,
through Maude Street mall, inside the empty
multi-storey car park, along High Street
to the railway station, down the Goulburn
Valley Highway to Kialla, up Railway
Parade past SPC, out New Dookie
Road to the abandoned abattoir.

We drank tinnies from eskies at the Deb
Ball in the Town Hall while mates escorted
local beauties, dove off the wooden stage
into each other's arms while the cover band
guitarist played the Wild Thing solo
with his teeth. Drank slabs of VB beside
the Broken River, Southern Comfort
in backyards, Carlton Draught at Detours,
the Vic and the Goulburn Valley Hotel.

I played basketball for the Demons,
reffed the under-12s for five bucks a game
while parents barracked and swore, delivered
newspapers, picked fruit during the summer
holidays, sold skateboards and clothes, fitted
gorgeous affluent classmates with rental
skis, boots, overalls, parkas and goggles.

I swam in irrigation channels,
held my breath beneath the railway bridge
as freight trains thundered above, played
tennis with my dad, got in fights outside
pubs, down at the shops, got bashed at housing
commission backyard end-of-school-year parties.

I was shunned at lunch, given the old hip
and shoulder while walking between classes,
shirtfronted during recess cricket,
survived bullies scrawling slurs on blackboards,
laughing abuse across basketball courts,
slamming my head against steel lockers,
angry at my earring, long hair, refusal
to conform to country town norms.

I climbed the observation tower, plunged
from a fraying rope swing into the muddy
Goulburn, unable to see the snags below.

Volume

Relaxing into a soft black leather
armchair inside the Bang & Olufsen
store at Camberwell Junction
I adjust headphones over teenage
ears, increase the volume, close my eyes
and experience U2's I Threw a Brick
Through a Window fully, completely.
Tom-toms, bass, snare and cymbals
boom, thunder, reverberate, crash,
echo inside my skull, rhythms transport
me from safe, leafy nineteen-eighties
upper-middle-class inner-south-eastern
Melbourne suburbia to nineteen-seventies
northside Dublin angst, rage and rebellion.

Port Fairy

Bluestone gutters line wide streets, fisherman's
cottages face each other, nets spread
across front yards. Norfolk Island pines shade

the caravan park. Beach house balconies
gaze out to sea. Dune grass rustles on sand.
Wild winter waves break against the lighthouse

on Griffiths Island near the ruins of piers,
cottages and a narrow-gauge railway.
Verandas cover bitumen footpaths

on Sackville Street. Nineteenth-century
bluestone banks and corner pubs with verandas
and balconies watch over volcanic rock.

A wooden bridge spans the Moyne. Fishing
boats rock beside the docks. The breakwater
stretches seaward from the river's mouth.

The bluestone state school on the hilltop looms
over the town. Church spires cast deep shadows.
Ancestor's bones lie in graves at town's edge.

Kids dangle hopeful fishing lines from docks
into the Moyne, hungrily tear open
sweaty packages of fish and chips wrapped

in butcher's paper, surf with mates, locals
at the East Beach, buy ice creams from the surf
lifesaving club kiosk, practice putting

in great-grandfathers' backyards, watch cricket
in great-grandmothers' houses, browse wetsuits
and custom boards in the surf shop, ride bikes

and skateboards down the Villiers Street hill,
buy bags of mixed lollies from the milk bar
across Princes Highway, watch Teen Wolf

at the cinema, conquer Galaga
in the takeaway, eat cornflakes with milk
and white sugar for breakfast, ride minibikes

in circles at the Christmas carnival,
pop ping-pong balls into oscillating clown
mouths, throw darts at balloons, aim too low.

Michael Quigley

Let us praise Michael Quigley
who crossed the seas by ship
from Ireland to Australia

Let us praise Michael Quigley
who swam two miles each morning
in the frigid Southern Ocean

and taught his four local-born
children to swim at Pea Soup
in the cool sheltered rock pools

Let us praise Michael Quigley
who drove a red bulldozer
for the state, helped create, carved

the Great Ocean Road through bush,
farmland, along cliff faces,
over hills, headlands and rivers

Let us praise Michael Quigley
who transported the songs
of Dublin to the Moyne banks

sat in his favourite armchair
playing She Moved Though the Fair
on his old harmonica

Let us praise Michael Quigley
for he built a six-foot-tall
bluestone wall around his land

on the hilltop with a view
of the ocean, surrounded
an acre of potatoes

Let us praise Michael Quigley
who taught his grandson to wield
a trowel, lay brick, smooth concrete

and carry his skills across
the ocean to a new home
repair crumbling foundations

Scarification

After Robbie Coburn & Michele Seminara's Scar to Scar

scars on my forehead
scars behind my ears
scars on my jawline
scars on my neck
scars on my back
scars on my forearms
scars on my knuckles
scars on my thumb
scars on my abdomen
scars on my thighs
scars on my kneecaps
scars on my shins
scars on my toes

long scars
short scars
deep scars
straight scars
curved scars
round scars
jagged scars

scarred by rugby
scarred by hernias
scarred by falling out of trees
scarred by diving off rocks
scarred by barbed wire fences
scarred by falling on a BBQ
scarred by surfing
scarred by skateboarding
scarred by backyard cricket
scarred by BMX racing
scarred by skin cancer
scarred by the surgeon's knife

Ritual

My aging father stands at the kitchen sink,
bent forward at the hips, sleeves rolled
to his elbows, washing cutlery, plates,
bowls and teacups by hand, where he has stood
every evening of my life. I whip
a tea towel from the drawer, take items
from the drying rack where Dad has placed
them after rinsing away lemon suds
in the second sink, shake hot water
off each plate, knife, fork, bowl or teacup,
dry them with a commemorative
tea towel, place them in the cupboard
or arrange them in the cutlery drawer.

As we wash and dry, Dad and I talk
about our lives, books we're reading, travel
plans, gardening, his deceased parents, friends,
teachers and students from our past lives,
our childhoods, politics, poetry
and the weather. Mum sits on the red velvet
couch in the lounge room beside the fireplace
knitting another jumper for one of her nine
grandchildren, using pure Aran wool
I bought for her in Galway,
while Van Morrison whispers in the corner.

III.

MOVEMENT

Freight Train

I can always hear a freight train
from beyond the cemetery
the rumble of wheels on steel
tracks carrying across the tomb-
stones, crosses and graves

I can always hear a freight train
from the east end of the street
traveling through live oaks
magnolias and crepe myrtles
over the traffic islands

I can always hear a freight train
under the gap beneath the window-
pane between the door and the frame
horn blowing before level crossings
blasting warnings through darkness

I can always hear a freight train
crossing the continent
negotiating the great divide
traversing the great plains
from Omaha to Cheyenne

I can always hear a freight train
reminding me of lost homes
absent loves, missed opportunities
boxcars not taken, doors never
forced open, wagons left empty

I can always hear a freight train
when I lie awake before dawn
remembering distant homelands
yearning to go back in time
act, move, love, risk, jump, fly, fall

I can always hear a freight train
moving oil, coal, steel and grain
echoing through the night
never letting me forget
there is always another journey

Inbetween Days

I run down empty streets each morning,
through a campus evacuated
of students and faculty, past vacant
classrooms, offices, cafeterias,

dorms, studios, galleries, performance
halls, the library, tennis courts, baseball,
lacrosse and soccer fields, the basketball
arena and the football stadium's

fifty thousand vacant seats. I run past
shuttered shops, empty houses of worship,
useless parking lots, shut-down malls, silent
restaurants, lifeless bars and coffee shops.

Back home I face a six-foot-wide window
at my five-foot-wide Scandinavian desk,
observe the yard and street between
Zoom meetings, online teaching, replying

to email, reading students' poetry,
essays and fiction, cancelling travel plans,
bugging airlines and hotels for refunds.
Blue jays perch each morning on the black iron

railing and mailbox outside my window.
Robins, cardinals, bluebirds and crows sing,
glide and feed in cleaner air. Lizards bask
on pedestrian-free sidewalks. Squirrels

scamper across empty lawns. The neighbors
on the corner paint their house white.
Audis, Volvos and Suburbans sit idle,
grow new coats of pollen and dust.

A stranded international student
rides his scooter up and down the street
like a leopard pacing an enclosure.
A white porcelain toilet sits beside

the curb, waiting for bulk trash pick-up
day. City workers cut excess boughs
from the live oaks shading the street, drag
limbs to the wood-chipper, grind life out

of branches and leaves. Pick-up trucks cruise
past, drivers' elbows protruding, searching
for salvageable furniture. We create
a new routine, check infection rates

and death tolls each morning, study curves
on graphs, practice social distancing,
cough into elbows, work remotely,
inspect expectorant, obsess over

the impossibility of testing,
decry government incompetence.
We mourn the absence of our previous
lives, cancelled travel, visits to parents.

We endure the loss of the newly
forbidden. Restaurants, bars, gyms and theatres
are closed. Festivals and readings cancelled.
St. Patrick's Day is cancelled. Weddings,

marathons, concerts, birthday parties
and family reunions—all cancelled
while we wait for the cure. Our future
cancelled, we retreat into well-known

corners, remodel bathrooms, paint walls
sky blue, install new light fixtures, trim
hedges, set up a backyard pool, clean out
the garage, saw off overhanging

branches from the neighbor's magnolia,
plant tomatoes, strawberries, rosemary,
kale, oregano and basil, dine
al fresco in the backyard. Walkers,

runners and cyclists emerge from lockdown,
strain themselves on traffic-less streets. Muscle

cars grind, scrape mufflers on the speedbump
hit at speed, drivers braking seconds too late.

A masked elderly couple stroll past
every afternoon, holding frail hands.

Chords & Lyrics

I pause *20,000 Days on Earth*
at eleven-fifteen as Nick Cave
works out chords & lyrics
to a new song at the piano
in his studio, walk to the kitchen
to refresh my gin & tonic, notice
a strip of golden light & D minor
emanating from beneath my daughter's
door. I turn the handle, push slowly
into the room to find her sitting cross-
legged on her bed, auburn hair hanging
down, working out chords & lyrics
on her grandfather's Gibson,
transforming & elevating.

Elsewhere

After Derek Mahon

Each morning I rise before dawn,
release Aslan out the back door,
shower, dress, breakfast,
drive my daughter to school,
walk streets lined with leafless
oaks in single-digit temperatures
to a campus with lush manicured
lawns and groomed flowerbeds
to teach privileged young minds
in comfortable heated classrooms.

Elsewhere, koalas, kangaroos,
echidnas and wallabies burn.
Family and friends don masks,
suck on Ventolin inhalers,
sweep ash from driveways,
choke on smoke suffocating
hometowns. Relatives evacuate
by boat, roads to escape cut
by fire, text photos across
the oceans of apocalyptic skies.

February

After Margaret Atwood

February, month of despair,
thank God for your relative brevity,
for an end to your twenty-eight
or twenty-nine bleak days of sub-zero
temperatures and minus-twenty windchills,
your blizzards, ice storms, snow dumps,
white-outs, mornings shovelling driveways,
melting ice from windshields and door handles
with jugs of warm water, pulling on layer
after layer of clothing before each excursion
outside the home or office, your short,
grey, frigid, miserable bastard days
lined with blackening piles of plowed
snow and torso-dissecting winds.
Fuck off February, and don't bother
coming back for another year.

International Arrivals

Loved ones, colleagues and limo drivers
crowd the space behind the barriers

waiting for flights to arrive
from Asia, Mexico, the Caribbean,

Europe and the Middle East.
Families sit at tables with coffee

or stand around in groups
holding helium balloons, flowers

and Welcome Home signs.
Limo drivers stand motionless

holding the names of clients
in front of their stomachs.

Restless kids squeal, skip,
run around and squirm.

Teenagers and adults occupy
their wait times with smartphones

looking up from screens
each time the automatic doors

open and passengers emerge
into the arrivals hall.

Groups of pilots and cabin crews
stride confidently through the doorway

ready for drinks at the hotel bar.
Business travelers walk directly

towards waiting drivers and shuttles.
Airline staff push elderly passengers

in wheelchairs with one hand,
tow luggage carts with the other.

Sunburnt families emerge wearing
hats, shorts and flip-flops,

scan the crowd for their ride.
Fathers push luggage carts

piled high with suitcases.
Mothers push strollers, hold kids'

hands tightly, issue instructions.
Waiting loved ones run towards

new arrivals, exchange kisses,
hugs and flowers, wipe away tears,

take luggage and hands, move
towards the exit with relief.

Sketchbook

For Celeste

a fish swims through
a black and white forest

a peacock with dice and cupcakes
in its tail glides across the page

three red wooden boats
ride waves on the ocean

a housecat with cheetah fur
guiltily eats raw meat

a robot named X100
waves her arms, yells *disco party!*

a golden retriever sits on a blanket
watching the sun set over the sea

a new breed of brown butterfly
is christened anmoreyetia

a headless torso with footless legs
sits in the middle of the page

a large-eyed Cyclops girl
stares down the viewer

a teddy bear with Wookie fur
looks forlornly to stage right

a Midnight Ball Princess exhibits
her braid for the viewer's admiration

cursive scrawled across two pages
proclaims   B   o   r   e   d !

a fluffy ginger cat sits atop
a compound word - mousefur

a faceless girl sits on a bench
beside a snowman beneath a tree

Asylum

They're dying to cross the border,
drowning in the Rio Grande
within reach of Texas, walking
fifteen-hundred miles in three months,
carrying toddlers on their backs,
sleeping in the desert, eluding
coyotes, thieves and kidnappers,
enduring hunger, fatigue, thirst,
assault, despair, indifference.
Walking all day, day after day,
week after week, month after month,
persisting beyond understanding
to seek asylum, shelter,
protection, the chance to live.
How can we ever turn away?

Virus as Metaphor

Here's how to look your best on a webcam.
More Americans should probably wear
masks for protection. In this moment

of solitude, books can be our passport
capturing a world of emptiness.
Global cases pass 600,000.

These dogs ooze personal style. Strangers
in an empty dorm. Why is America
choosing mass unemployment? This is the fate

of an undocumented immigrant.
Cuomo dismisses Trump's idea for NY
region quarantine. It's grim out there.

America stress-bought all the baby
chickens. Learn how to access the data,
the shock felt by millions of unemployed

Americans alone on the road.
Rational panic, but also rational
hope, when the mundane becomes heroic.

Virus as metaphor. It's time to talk
about death, weaving a way out
of isolation. Death tolls in Europe

surge. Boris Johnson should have taken
his own medicine. Bob Dylan's
seventeen-minute surprise. The Nordic

way to economic rescue. U.S.
enacts largest relief package
in modern history. What should you do

about your babysitter during
coronavirus? We have a lot
of ideas about what to read.

Some U.S. cities could have outbreaks worse
than Wuhan's. Trump signs $2 Trillion Dollar
Bill. Crepes don't have to be fancy to be

delicious. Courage inside a Brooklyn
hospital. You are your safest sex partner.
Turn the living room into a stage. Check

is in the mail? Head to the kitchen
and bake. What we can learn from European
dog culture. The perfect window

for a first impression. Be more productive
in seven days. Trump chooses disaster
as his re-election strategy.

U.S. price gouging complaints surge amid
pandemic. Let's kick coronavirus's
ass. Now is the time to take care of your

lungs. Living near train tracks they survived
Spanish Flu, the Depression and the Holocaust.
Locked out of the virtual classroom. Take

the tidy home challenge. It's too late
to avoid disaster. Your new social-
distancing workout. Can the restaurant

industry survive? Studies suggest
the virus can cross the placenta. Should
we stay or should we go? Bring in the robot

cleaners. Surging traffic is slowing down
our internet. Then the world turned upside
down in praise of a normal, boring country.

In this emergency, mom knows best.
What's the best fix for a recession?
A silent spring is saying something.

Virus costs university students
a rite of passage. I am hospitalized.
The fourth wall is my laptop screen.

Profit

Bulldozers and graders destroy
live oaks and mesquite, push
out the suburban edge, annihilate
nature to create new streets
and cleared flat building lots
awaiting construction of homes
adjacent to schools, capitalizing
on location, maximizing property
values and tax revenues for the city.
Capitalism obliterates everything
that cannot be monetized, kills
the trees, grass and wildflowers,
destroys habitats and ecosystems
in relentless pursuit of return.

Bookpeople

For Celeste

Bookstore browsing
we begin with *Harry Potter*
discuss the merits
of various cover art
before moving on to *Star Wars*
crafts and *Percy Jackson*

finally, it's Dad's turn
so we descend the stairs
to Poetry and Fiction
break for bagels and coffee
with *Quidditch Through the Ages*
and Charles Wright's *Caribou*
before finishing with journals
magazines, fridge magnets
wands and horcruxes

Trail Ride

meet Bart and Pecos Jimmy
at the end of the dirt road

eight thousand feet above
sea level, higher than Kosciuszko

chat about forest fires
bear sightings and snowfall

while horses and cowboys
are watered, tighten saddles

adjust stirrups for each rider
before mounting and setting

off across the high meadow
fluttering with golden, white

black and monarch butterflies
ride single file into the forest

weaving upwards through
birch, ponderosa and aspen

always climbing and watching
blue skies above mountains

face-height branches flicking
fallen logs under hooves

daughter's bare legs gripping
leather and smooth brown flanks

bare feet resting in cool stirrups
wind blowing sun-lightened hair

Holy Ghost

follow Holy Ghost Creek
higher towards its source

keep the water on your right
and the mountain on your left

cross the creek on fallen logs
follow the path that guides you

teach your daughter to make
stones walk on the water

Mountain Forest Campground

pitch the tent beside the river
listen to the rushing water
all day and all night
always the rushing water
even in dreams

sit at a picnic table
in the shade of the pines
eight thousand feet
above sea level
eat drink read write

brew coffee over an open fire
chop wood and carry water
sit in the darkness
beside the fire
and simply exist

listen to your fellow camper
with the grey ponytail
blow his sax
all through the slow afternoon
beside his caravan
hope that one of these days
he plays Van's Caravan

watch the pines sway
in the evening breeze
breathe in the pine
listen to the wind
merge with rushing water

WWJD?

At the Cisco Travel Plaza
Jesus Camp kids wearing blue
t-shirts with FUMCW2016
emblazoned on the front
and *GO!* on the back swamp
restrooms, block drink fridge
doors, crowd candy aisles,
form queues snaking away
from cash registers,
wait to pay with armfuls
of drinks, candy and chips.

A blonde, blue-eyed Jesus
Camp girl lacking the patience
of a saint arrives at the congregation
of disciples waiting to pay, declares
OH MY GOD! YOU'VE GOT
TO BE KIDDING ME. TELL ME
THIS ISN'T THE LINE?!

Komatsu

The bright yellow
bulldozer awaits amidst
eager acres of dirt

I step on to the blade
across to the tracks
climb into the cab

fasten seatbelt, start engine
turn throttle to max
release safety shut-off levers

grip joysticks in each hand
raise blade with my right
shift gears with my left

rumble forward in my twenty-
tonne earthmoving beast
feeling power over landscape

reaching my target, I press
the deceleration pedal
with my right foot, roll to a halt

pushing the joystick forward
I lower the blade, change gears
push the earth in front of me

stop, raise the blade, reverse
repeat process again
and again as my hillock grows

satisfied with my creation
I drive up and over the earth
spin one hundred and eighty

degrees, drop the blade once
more, doze earth back into place
grade surface smooth and depart

The Suburb of the Future

Purchase your dream home today!
Homes start in the low 300s.
A variety of floorplans let you choose

homes from three thousand to four thousand
square feet. You can choose from three,
four or five bedroom floorplans.

Our homes come with double or triple
garages. We have both single and double
story options, many with bonus rooms!

YOU get to decide. We have homes to suit
YOUR lifestyle. Conveniently located
between major freeways, Interstates

and tollways. Easy access to employment
hubs, education and play! Your new home
is just exits away from the airport, retail,

entertainment and a range of dining options,
including fast food and family restaurants—
Outback Steakhouse, Texas Roadhouse

and Salt Lick BBQ just to name a few!
Become part of the Next Great Neighborhood.
Our development includes world-class

modern infrastructure pre-installed.
Our carefully selected award-winning
builders create inspired architecture.

Come and grow your family
with us. Enhance your life today!

Duck Feast

The maintenance workers race
their tool-laden golf cart
to the water's edge, orange step-
ladder rattling on the back, park
beside Willow Lake, climb out
and toss freshly-torn chunks
of white bread to the ducks
swimming towards the grassy shore.
The bearded, overweight middle-
aged men, clad in black baseball
caps, navy fleece jackets and khaki
cargo pants, stand facing the water,
call the ducks, throw bread underarm
to the gathering flock, squat
on haunches to summon dozens
of Mallards and their black and white
brethren. Richard attempts a frisbee-
style side-arm while Dale replicates
Little League pitches. The bread
spent, the men stand for minutes
with hands in pockets, clucking
and whistling, observe the feast,
climb back into the cart,
drive away to waiting work.

White Privilege

concrete paths red brick pavers circle sculpture
pedestal manicured hedges bikes rack parked

gravel echoes hammer hitting steel admin building
under construction casts shadows over lawn

crepe myrtles line paths donor's names carved
stone above entrances students faculty stroll

past campus police chat in parked golf cart
doors automatic open air-conditioned space

students wait at tables under umbrellas
gravel crunches underfoot breezes sway boughs

columns flank doorways worker delivers box
printer paper hand trolley rumble flip flops flick

concrete hazard lights generator flash parked
FedEx truck wind lifts students' hair dragonflies

dart hedge to hedge vehicles rev keys jangle
accelerate on university drive

bike wheels whir truck engines idle citrus scent
perfume shampoo white clouds streak blue sky

hand slides along rail silver ring scrapes metal
buttocks rest black bench fallen leaves twigs decompose

on gravel students exit buildings in swarms
footsteps follow smooth swept sunlit concrete paths

insects settle on students' hairy forearms
follow shadows purple flowers bounce treetops

windows reflect buildings cream brick faces off
prospective students parents pass campus tours

student guides lead backwards cowboy boots skirt
twin prop plane passes overhead campus police

cruise past SUV electric hedge trimmers
buzz outside dorms students text walking block foot

traffic keys jingle swinging lanyards pink straps
dangle backpacks squirrels scurry trunks sneakers

scuff concrete trucks honk pedestrian crossings
airbrakes hiss luggage wheels click concrete gaps

clouds reflect classroom windows passenger
jet passes high above muted roar pedals

rotating click wheeled bikes students sneeze
beneath magnolias laptops rest crossed legs

metal bench hydroflask tings westerly blows hair
leaves descend into shrubbery heat emanates

sculptures flags ripple atop poles landscapers'
trailers bounce student wheels scooter left-handed

clutches coffee passing students cough landscaper
wears broad-brimmed straw hat dark-green trousers

light-green shirt sculpts hedges trims shrubs ginger-haired
man mustard shirt strolls past helicopter chops sky

above red-tiled roofs young man evades bee on lawn
blinds drawn behind west-facing windows

landscapers recline in shade of crepe myrtles
dragonflies dive bank dart clouds drift slowly north-

east freight train horn blares in the distance faculty chat
sidewalk outside building rectangular bricks

interlock wave patterns construction dates carved
in stone ferns shelter beneath live oaks backpacks

rest beside feet pink roses purple t-shirts white
shorts black yoga pants floodlights attached to tree

limbs acorns crunch underfoot girl with butterfly
tattoo young man dreadlocked crowds wait crossing

Adjustment

JETLAG: spending the early hours
of the morning reading *The Only
White Landscape;* re-organizing
books on the shelves in the study;
updating lists of books to read
and books read; wondering why
the sleeping pills don't work;
reading about Trump's latest
abominations, false statements,
lies and distortions; learning
the details of the Paris Climate
Change Accord; trying hard
to be quiet, to not wake the family;
hoping sleep comes before dawn.

Preparations for the Fourth

mow and edge the front
and back lawns, weed flowerbeds
and cracks between paved areas

scrub the BBQ grill and wash
cooking implements
add fresh water to the pond

sweep the front porch
and the back verandah
add chemicals to the hot tub

drive to the store
and purchase a gas canister
refill, hamburger patties, buns

sausages, tortilla chips, avocado
onion, lime, tomatoes
fruit drinks for the kids

cerveza, gin, tonic and fireworks
stock the outdoor fridge
create a retro party playlist

prepare for blatant displays
of xenophobia
and narrow-minded patriotism

External Composition

Ground gravel quartz sparkles. Broken
glass chips intermingle. Shadows
of leaves and branches oscillate. Wind

re-arranges hair and clothing. Students
sit cross-legged on manicured lawns,
notebooks resting on knees, knuckles

gripping pens and pencils, pages rustling,
eyes focused on text. Cream-brick buildings
reflect in each other's windows on opposite

sides of the quad. Magnolia branches bounce
and sway above trimmed hedges with ninety-
degree angles. Porticos rest on Corinthian

columns above ground-level entrances.
Naked boughs of crepe myrtles reach
skyward towards celestial skies streaked

with transparent clouds while a private jet
migrates across the blue. Students amble
in pairs and solitude along concrete paths

towards coffee, class, the library, a late lunch
or The Pub. Delivery trucks idle at driveway's
end beneath spreading live oak limbs.

A bee flies slowly from magnolia to lawn
following its internal GPS. Students pull
iPhones from pockets, focus on screens

while shuffling, heads bowed in worship.

Acorns

A squirrel and a crow
fight on the lawn,
competing for acorns.

The squirrel runs and leaps
at the crow; the crow beats
its wings, elevates up and back.

The victor ignores the vanquished,
burrows its head into the lawn, feasting.

Reprieve

At twelve twenty-five on a Saturday
I walk east in my laceless Converse
from the Discount Tire store on the I-20
frontage road, my bank balance four-
hundred and ninety dollars lower, uphill
through the vacant lot, climb over rocks,
step around cactus through dry brown
grass past empty thirty-two-ounce Styrofoam
Whataburger cups, a prone For Lease sign
and tangles of Texas barbed wire, through
the strip mall parking lot by Mattress Firm,
the Cotton Patch Café and Great Clips,
across expanses of cracked concrete baking
in ninety-seven-degree heat to the Starbucks
on South Main, seeking iced coffee, Siggi's
Icelandic skyr, a reprieve from Texas
summer heat and a quiet place to read
poetry, listen to Pearl Jam, peruse the latest
report on the India v. England test match,
check email, scroll through Facebook, Instagram
and Twitter, catch up on the lives of family,
friends, colleagues and strangers
while bearded, tattooed workers in grey
shorts, shirts and caps install four new tires.

Lake Effects

The lights on the shoreline
surround Willow Lake, cast
soft light across water.

Nineteen beams point towards
my window, silver and gold
bobbing on the surface

as wind creates ripples
from southwest to northeast.
The fountain in the lake's

centre spurts jets fifteen
feet skyward, the water
arcing, falling over

a six-foot-high three-hundred-
and-sixty-degree spray
like an inverted liquid

umbrella, the display
illuminated from below
by floodlights aimed at stars.

The jets rise and fall,
pulse in perfect rhythm
like a pumping organ,

their mist blown northeast. Twelve
mallards and eight white swans
settle down for the night,

heads tucked under quiet wings,
while houses on the farther
shore darken as midnight falls.

Campus Events

The FedEx truck speeds uphill past
the indoor football practice facility,
brakes squeakily at the four-way stop.

A skateboarder glides past classroom
windows, urethane wheels smacking joints
between concrete slabs, sending rhythmic

soundwaves between windowpanes.
City workers station orange cones
in rows on University Drive, redirect

traffic around a burst water main.
Escaping gallons spew across white lines,
cascade along gutters, immerse crosswalks,

arc from tires of speeding trucks and SUVs.
Tardy students step lightly through shallow
puddles, dodging deeper dirty water,

seeking to avoid saturation. The workers
shout instructions in español over rumbling
backhoes and water pumps, high-pitched
beeping of reversing dump trucks.

Rainwater

Rain falls flooding the backyard.
The pond overflows.
Drops drip from the trumpet vine.

The circular paved dining
area an inch-
deep pool, the overgrown lawn

yearns for the lawnmower's blade.
Peach trees bend towards
the earth. Drops bead upon strings

of outdoor party lights. Steam
rises from beneath
the edges of the hot tub

cover. The wheelbarrow fills
to its rusty brim.
Rainwater glazes the grill.

Lego Building

For Celeste

dump the bucket's contents
out on the bedroom carpet

turn your doll's bed upside down
to create a flat building surface

consult with your co-creator
about today's custom build

divide tasks evenly and fairly
lay down the baseplates

create separate piles of pieces
organized by color, rake

and sift through the big pile
looking for green, brown, tan

grey, blue and white pieces
set all mini figures aside

combine Friends, Harry Potter
and Star Wars sets together

into new creations, organized
according to new principles

throw away the instruction
manuals, listen to inspiration

create your own new world
built upon your own dreams

Protection/Prevention

please use other entrance use the stairs
if you are able fulfill your potential
come join us bible study condom carnival
explore your options trivia night! mask up!
maintain your distance protect our campus
planetarium physics and chemistry FIRE
EXTINGUISHER maintain a distance
of eight steps from others on the stairs
EXIT discharge ground floor do you need help?
you are not alone protect yourself and others
stand here! no matter the distance you can still get
involved protect yourself! protect the herd!
free flu shots in the health center disposable
face masks when on campus you must
wear a face covering health promotion
substance abuse events POSTER SALE
TODAY! ASSISTANCE ELECTRICAL
stand in designated corners coronavirus
prevention EXIT STAIRS EXIT

Notes & Feedback

Distorted notes & feedback roar from my daughter's room;
soundwaves travel through the wall, vibrate framed art.
The Seven Nation Army riff explodes the gloom.

She sits cross-legged before her amp, wears her costume:
black Docs, black jeans, t-shirt with the words of Descartes.
Distorted notes & feedback roar from my daughter's room.

She increases the volume, makes Meg White's drums boom.
Plays the notes over and over, repeatedly hits restart.
The Seven Nation Army riff explodes the gloom.

She amplifies bass & treble, works to exhume
the groove, searches for sublime changes to impart.
Distorted notes & feedback roar from my daughter's room.

Her Strat charges the air with audio perfume.
The song crescendos, she returns to the start.
The Seven Nation Army riff explodes the gloom.

I sit & listen, drum on my desk, hear her bloom,
savor the sounds, dread the day she will depart.
Distorted notes & feedback roar from my daughter's room;
the Seven Nation Army riff explodes the gloom.

Summer Rain

arrives before sunset

    lowers the temperature

        pours from the eaves

            fills the water feature

                spears into the dirt

                    pools in the flower beds

                        makes green grass glow

soaks outdoor furniture

    runs down the driveway

        drums on the window

            drowns out the radio

                turns grey fences brown

                    washes gutters clean

                        glistens like quartz

Departed

we sat in bed on a Thursday
afternoon, held hands while we watched

Perseverance land on Mars, seek
the *sands of past life,* heard NASA

scientists whoop and holler, high-
five each other, marveled at images

transmitted from the red planet
back to our pale blue dot, listened

to the sounds of a distant sphere
traveling to our town, wondered

if we might be the last to find
the evidence of life departed

IV.

MIDDLE EIGHT

Manifestations

I urge like a red lacquered
fingernail tapping a car
window, rat-tat-tating, exclaiming
over there! faster than words

I erupt like Fagradalsfjall
ejecting lava, transforming landscape
blending fire with the northern lights
attracting crowds of photographers

I insist like mustard stains
on sky blue trousers, draw eyes
to upper thighs, inner seams
announce my unwanted presence

I blister like Irish skin
left too long in Australian sun
swell, burst, ravage, create
carcinomas, scar and heal

A Prayer to Nick Cave

Nick
Cave, black
bard of Brighton
Berlin, Sao Paulo, Melbourne
and Wangaratta, composer of darkness

show us beauty and mystery, guide
us like Charon down the treacherous rivers
of our memories, imagination and desires, grant passage
to self-knowledge, the lime-tree arbour of art

Good Friday, 1930

Hundreds of millions of worshippers
attended church services around
the world, commemorating Jesus'
crucifixion and death at Calvary.
Believers fasted, wept, knelt, sang, prayed.
Schools, universities, offices
and shops closed. There is no news today.

Rebels fighting for independence
from harsh British colonial rule,
inspired by the 1916
Irish Easter rising, burned armouries
in Bengal. The administration
imposed martial law. British troops restored
order. There is no news today.

The *Salt Lake Telegram* reports Mrs.
Sarah Robinson Rushton, mother
of two sons and six daughters, fifty-
seven grandchildren, eighty-six great-
grandchildren, and eight great-great-grand-
children, died aged ninety-three of general
debility. There is no news today.

Dolores Caplinger was born
in Virginia. Dolores Black,
Dolores Hollenbach and Dolores
Boring were born in Pennsylvania.
Dolores Gamel was born in New
York. Dolores Rogers was born
in Ohio. There is no news today.

An eighteenth-century wooden church
caught fire in Costeşti, Romania,
during Easter mass. The roof collapsed.
The narrow door jammed. One hundred
and eighteen souls perished, all but two
children and teens. Fourteen escaped
alive. There is no news today.

Warhol

Andy watches over
the gallery mouth
slightly open black
eyes straight ahead

cheeks sunken hair
standing straight
up spiking and falling
over black eyebrows

ears shadow-hidden
his green face lunges
forward out of darkness
surveying polished concrete

walls floors stairs
observing visitors
arriving to gaze
upon his image

Wheat Work

after Pieter Bruegal's The Harvesters *(1565)*

In the field on the hillside above
our village, we cut ripe yellow stalks,
stack late summer wheat, construct ricks, swing
scythes while Jan sleeps sprawled beneath the pear
tree, shirking work. Women take their turn
to lunch on bread, milk and pears, seated
on benches of freshly-cut golden
grain. Others carry bundles downhill
through the wheat corridor while we scythe.
In the green lane below our fertile
field the wagon stacked high with harvest
prepares to drive to the bay where ships
wait to transport wheat to hungry shores.

Sweet Movement

I want to glide across the floor with you,
ride gently upon waves of sound with you.

We scale heights when you
float, turn, bend and groove with me.
Please don't dance alone,
baby. Craft rhythm with me.

I sustain yearning notes with you,
touch beauty and surrender with you.

Create harmony, baby.
Orchestrate my admiration, do.
Draw my sweet movement to you.

I embrace minor chords for you,
reach climax and dénouement with you.

Caress chords and notes, baby,
rise and swell with fascination, do.
Draw my sweet movement to you.

Preparation

A toned man stands at the counter
in his kitchen, pink shirt-sleeves rolled,
spoons white sugar into highball
glasses, adds twelve mint leaves, cuts lime
into wedges, squeezes fresh juice
over sugar, pulverizes
mint, tongs ice cubes into each glass,
pours a stream of white Cuban rum,
tops off the drink with soda water,
stirs vigorously with a cocktail
stick. Waiting for the doorbell to chime
he memorizes his amorous
pitch, hopes for an erotic tryst,
convinces himself she won't flinch.

Lodestars

A framed black and white portrait
of my Irish great-great-great-
grandfather hangs on the wall
like an icon in a Russian church.
Trad tunes bind me to ancestors,
lodestars shepherding me back
home after generations in exile,
piloting me across decades
and hemispheres to green fields,
forests, loughs, hills, hedgerows,
cliffs, beaches, islands, villages,
rivers, kitchens and hearths warm
as whiskey, comforting as soda
bread, familiar as the dark
snug in my ancestors' local.

V.

INTERLUDE

Homecoming

We arrived in Cavan by bus
from Carrickmacross, walked

from the Bus Eireann station
to Sweelan Lough, pitched our burgundy

tent beneath the trees behind
the green hedges beside the cool

water, walked back into the town
centre along Kilnavarragh

Road, Wolfe Tone and Bridge streets, withdrew
punts from Ulster Bank, walked up the town past

the Church of Ireland to the Cathedral
of Saints Patrick and Felim, knelt

in a wooden pew, whispered prayers
and lit candles for my Bréifne

ancestors, strolled hand in hand back down
Church and Main, settled in for a long slow

evening in Percy's Bar at the Farnham
Arms, sipped Guinness, feasted on chips,

soup, soda bread, potatoes and salmon,
sang folk songs with newfound friends,

warmed ourselves in the welcome home,
sank into the comfort of dark wood,

scarlet ceilings and soft golden lamps,
stumbled out the door at closing time

with arms around each other's shoulders,
wove our way back to the tent, kicked

off boots, stripped off clothes, wriggled
naked into sleeping bags zipped together.

Townland

For Patrick O'Reilly (1835-1903)

As a young man in my native townland
of Kinnea, I walked across sunset fields
between hedgerows to her open door,
settled down beside her peatsmoke fire,
sipped whiskey, allowed myself to study
her beauty, hoped life would never change.

The autumn leaves began to change,
brought auburn and orange to the townland.
We walked on the drumlins to study
the lowering sky, gazed over fields
where our ancestors ploughed, rained fire
on invaders, barricaded the door.

When neighbours knocked on my midnight door
with an urgent warning, I was forced to change.
Necessity poured water on my fire,
drove me in desperation from the townland
of my birth, across the emerald fields,
over the ocean into exile to study

longing. I devoted myself to study
distance and departure, discovered the door
to return to my beloved Kinnea fields.
Decades of lonely work enabled change,
brought me home to my beloved townland,
restored me to my own hearth and fire.

I sit alone and grey, tend my fire,
savour whiskey, write my story, study
the history of my county and townland.
I strip, sand and repaint my green door,
make preparations for belated change,
welcome new flocks into my fields.

Lambs bleat and frolic in my lush fields,
graze beside their mothers beneath the fire
of the Bealtaine sunset. Late life change

brings autumn pleasures, inspires study.
At midnight on Samhain I pass out the door,
walk the boreens of my beloved townland.

A change approaches. I remember. I study
the past, the fire that drew me to her door.
Bury me in the fields of my dear townland.

Pilgrimage

At the counter of a coffee shop
across the street from St. Stephen's Green
on the saint's day, an old lady mistakes
me for a local, tries to start a conversation
about the best cake shops in Dublin.
I apologize for my ignorance,
turn to my espresso and lemon cake.

I sit alone in a booth with a pint
at the International Bar waiting
for my old mate to arrive from Paris.
I admire the ceilings, marble bar
and stained-glass windows, shiver despite
my merino and coat. I share the space
with twelve other men, aged between eighteen
and eighty. On the TV, West Ham leads Fulham
2-1 early in the second half. I study
the tiled floor, peruse the whiskey collection
on the back bar, order a roast beef sandwich.

We visit my grandfather's birthplace and childhood
home on Nash Street in Inchicore, drink pints
at The Black Horse, my great-grandfather's local,
are too slow to catch Christy the paralytic
as he falls sideways across the stools
onto the radiator, ribs-first. We lift
and seat him in a chair, ask after his health.
The bartender calls a cab, delivers him home.

July Evening

After Patrick Kavanagh

Leave Stradeen in the late afternoon, walk
north past Kelly's to the Inniskeen road.
Step northeast between hedgerows, walls and fields
towards Inniskeen, breathless with desire,
cross the invisible border between
Monaghan and Louth, cross back a quarter
mile later, pass the GAA pitches
and Mary Mother of Mercy. Press on
to Deery's Terrace, the playground, Duffy's,
Riverside, Saint Daigh's, through the village past
Sean's to the Patrick Kavanagh Centre
and meet Bernadette as she locks the doors.
Stroll hand in hand through the blooming evening
catching light dancing in her auburn hair.

Field Work

Suck three deep breaths. Open your bloody jaw
wide. Hold the inhaler to your lips. Spray
three bursts of Ventolin into your mouth.
Swallow the cool blue aerosol. Assess
the situation before rushing back
onto the field to pack down at the rear
of the scrum. Snatch the ball from underfoot,
burst to your left past the blindside flanker,
cut right, stiff-arm your opposite number,
revel in schadenfreude as he falls
backwards onto the turf, slalom between
the closing right winger and the fullback,
sprint across the white twenty-two-yard line
towards the corner flag and victory.

Sanctuary

For Jessica Traynor

Treeless grassed hills
divided by drystone walls
sculpted by salted winds
slate-roofed cottages
scattered across landscape
sheep huddling beside
hedgerows in the drizzle

The logs in the fireplace
spit and crackle, flames
ebb, rise on wind
gusting down the chimney
heat emanates from the hearth
defrosts farmer's fingers
fresh from feeding cattle

An elderly man stands
broad back to the window
gnarled hands spread
above the orange flames
bent forward at the hips
drawn towards warmth
in late-January darkness

VI.

CRESCENDO

Confession

I got drunk alone in Islington, drank
pint after pint of bitter, overwhelmed
by homesickness and loneliness, descended
deeper and deeper into the darkness
of myself like a worker lowered
by ropes into a bottomless well,
sat on a wooden stool at the bar,
ignored Shane McGowan drinking pints
of vodka and tonic in the corner,
let my head sink towards my chest,
shoulders slump. I exchanged ten quid
in the toilets for a small plastic bag
of white powder, decided to get
me a little oblivion. Out
on Upper Street I stumbled south-southeast
towards Angel, bought an international
calling card from a South Asian newsagent,
found a phone booth with shattered glass,
called a dear friend in another time zone,
confessed my sins, received forgiveness.

Safe Home

After alighting from the Paddington
train at one AM, I stroll quiet, near-
empty streets through crisp Autumn air, flaneur
Dorchester, Southgate, St. James's Parade
and Monmouth. On the Upper Bristol Road,
heading for Royal Victoria Park,
I approach a woman wearing a black
dress walking barefoot, carrying red heels.
As my long strides bring me closer, I hear
her crying, see her white shoulders heave
as she sobs, passes beneath weak streetlights,
through shadows of Georgian buildings. I slow,
switch to the north side of the road, fall back
the length of a cricket pitch, watch her home.

Marching

A few blocks from the Duomo
two rows of riot police
carrying helmets and shields

force me to step out
of the narrow street
into a doorway, stand aside

as hundreds of chanting protesters
march past carrying banners, placards
and a replica of the Italian constitution

prone on a stretcher.
Locals and tourists en route
to restaurants wait in doorways

silently observing, taking photographs
of the marchers and rows
of armed police following

the tail and two armoured vans,
blue lights flashing, ready
to whisk human cargo away.

Dark Angel

The waitress balances
plates on her wrist

glides between tables
bar and kitchen

dressed in black
jokes with customers

earns her wages
like a prima ballerina

the dark angel at my table
calls out orders and farewells

Antonio! Duo caffe! Prego
Bianco Toscana

Aqua naturale, grazie
Cappuccino, per favore

Ciao grazie, signora
Ciao ciao, domani

Florentine Discourse

I'm in the zone, let me be
I prefer non-denominational

I'm well-travelled and well-educated
no one wants to know anything about you

it was totally reasonable to tell us to be quiet
and then it got really awkward

she's really New York
I didn't realize she had broken

up with her boyfriend
mozzarella – that's so Italian

she broke up with him over text
after two and a half years

it's like the Mason situation
every time she has sex she goes to confession

and thinks it erases it like whatever
my dad was forced to go to church

there are Pinocchios here
I should have told him about the bargaining

coffee! *cappuccino!*
hey babe, take a walk on the wild side

everything alright here?
oh what service!

what was the other thing he gave you?
red wine, yes

I have a table over there, right?
the toilets are in the back on the left

fantastic, thank you
prego, grazie

Santa Maria Maggiore

Soldiers with machine guns stand guard outside the Basilica,
check visitors' bags for weapons. Pilgrims and tourists arch
necks back to gaze upon majestic ornate ceilings inlayed
with gold. Forty fluted marble columns gesture towards
heaven, twenty-six arched windows bathe the interior
with celestial light. Marble angels hold up gold-framed
oil paintings depicting scenes of beauty and fear, Mary
with Baby Jesus, Moses with the Ten Commandments,
Jesus stretched upon the cross. Feet shuffle across acres
of cool floor, white and grey marble crafted in spirals, squares
and rectangles. Sandal soles slap gently against bare heels.
Fourteen priests sit in booths hearing confessions in Italian,
French, Spanish, Dutch, Polish, Hungarian, Czech, Russian,
English, German and Slovak. Gated chapels occupy
the wings. Worshippers kneel and cross themselves before a holy
relic: wood from Jesus' crib. Marble child angels observe
the crowds. Red velvet chairs wait behind the altar.
The Basilica hums with the murmur of conversations.
A choir sings in Latin beneath scarlet, gold, blue, green
and orange arches, domes, stars, crests and laurels. A priest
hushes tourists from an open confessional. Euro
are exchanged for candles and blessings. A marble pope kneels
beneath saints and martyrs. Bells toll. Latin inscriptions adorn
floors, walls and ceilings. Red candles burn in golden
candelabras. Velvet ropes deny access to holy spaces.
Adoring worshippers kneel before a golden cross
on the altar. An ambulance siren beseeches
from Via dell'Esquilino. Recessed floodlights
illuminate mahogany confessionals and polished
benches. A white-robed priest reads alone in a booth. Roman
numerals immortalize dates of birth and death, lengths of reigns.
A baby crawls across the marble floor as the organ crescendos.
Nuns in white, blue and black habits take photos
with smartphones of naked torsos, bare breasts, golden hair,
anguished faces dominated by fear of punishment.

Homesickness (Remix)

For Christodoulos Makris

I don't think we should panic
I'm not an outright failure

Copenhagen-style urban
density for Generation Z

buttonholed him there
the Dutch long-term planning

designing for energy efficiency
big mama rat won't let go

education through diversity
not an outright failure

on a sinking ship brutal
homesickness attention

throwing myself off the ship
impossible to fit function

comfort and lifecycle
rank high in the priorities

proper dialogue integration
concrete is more than carbon

too much monologue attention
climate resilience music

you get that from travelling
brutal homesickness

impossible round hole
never going to be properly

famous square peg branding
when you're away you think

much more function
needs less maintenance attention

lasts much longer integrated
image in my mind impossible

seriously diminished generation
exposed timber doesn't wear well

I don't think we should panic
a level of sophistication

to engage in dialogue
throwing myself off the ship

impossible to fit homesickness
I'm not an outright failure

comfort and lifecycle rank
concrete is more brutal music

too much monologue you get
that from travelling certain

countries urban density
buttonholed him longterm

planning big mama rat
never going branding

when you're away won't let go
designing you think

outright failure sinking ship
proper dialogue less maintenance

diversity priorities carbon
climate properly famous

square peg resilience
sophistication seriously diminished

engage Copenhagen-style
exposed timber brutal

homesickness energy efficiency
education image lasts much

longer dialogue doesn't wear well
big mama rat I don't think we should

panic on a sinking ship climate

Playa Tortugas

Couples wrestle in blue hotel pools
beside palms bent groundward by hurricanes.

Brown women in bikinis pose on white sand
for photos. Pink jet skis carve clear water.

Catamarans cruise to Isla Mujeras.
Red buses surge along the boulevard.

Twisted roofing iron splays in vacant lots.
Blue mesh loungers recline on white sand.

Palm trees enfold red-tiled roofs. Fifty high-
rise hotels populate the peninsula.

Forty-three moored boats sway at the marina.
Honeymooning couples promenade the playa.

Debris sprinkles flat white rooftops. Palms
girdle ochre and green tennis courts.

Speed boats carve figure eights in turquoise.
Uniformed hotel workers wait at bus stops.

A swimsuit blown from a balcony rests
on a flat rooftop seven floors below.

Dark grey thunderclouds loiter above orange
buoys marking the edge of the swimming zone.

Police SUVs and ambulances
speed east on the boulevard, lights flaring.

Seagulls soar on the wind. Sirens call.
Luxury villas retreat behind concrete

walls. Lizards laze across the sidewalk. Vendors
stroll the playa, beseech vacationers -

Hey boss! Hola! Tattoo? Coconut water?
Sombrero? Mojito? Cerveza, piña

colada, tequila, margarita?—
while touts promote tours—*You want dinner cruise?*

Swim with dolphins? Snorkeling? Catamaran?
Pirate ship sunset? Romantic massage?

Taxi drivers lean against hoods smoking
cigarettes. A woman in a bikini

kneels on a balcony facing the sun.
A thirty-foot cruiser docks at the pier,

disgorges affluent cargo while palm
fronds bounce and sway in the easterly.

Air-conditioning units roar. Streetlights
flicker on fifteen minutes before sunset.

A hotel worker drags a forty-gallon
black garbage bag along a dirt path towards

the edge of the compound. The Isla
Mujeres ferry sounds its mournful horn.

Drizzle blows west across the Caribbean
Sea. January swell rises. The chop picks

up. A baby cries two floors above. Palm
trees bend westwards. Moisture coats balcony

tiles. The lime scent of shrimp ceviche drifts
up from the restaurant below. Floating

trampolines and inflatable slides bob
above sapphire water. Air brakes hiss and sigh.

Humid diagonal rain lashes down
at sunset, drives all bodies to shelter.

VII.

CODA

Crossings

I.
dart like a javelina
between mesquite and boulders
run beside the Rio Grande
through Big Bend National Park

II.
spend hours absorbed in the woods
near Bath hiking the skyline trail
see nobody awake
on frosty autumn mornings

III.
run southeast beside the blue
waters of Port Phillip Bay
from the Port Melbourne
War Memorial to St. Kilda
Pier thawing in bright winter
morning sunshine, look south-
southwest towards Rosebud
remember journeys taken
in long-forgotten lifetimes

After the Pandemic

Hike from Avebury to Stonehenge
via Hilcott. Circumnavigate
Inis Mór on mountain bikes. Stop

at Dún Aonghasa to lie on the cliff's
edge high above the blue Atlantic.
Climb Croagh Patrick. Survey Clew Bay

from Clare to Achill. Drink golden
lager in summer sunshine outside
Haddington House in Dún Laoghaire.

Sing along with the crowd in The Dame
Tavern. Ride the train from Dublin
to Galway. Drive the Wild Atlantic

Way from Donegal to Dingle.
Stroll rainy twilight Soho streets,
blend into Glastonbury crowds.

Flaneur the streets of Reykjavik,
meditate in Hallgrimskirkja.
Browse Melbourne bookstores, sip espresso

alfresco on Lygon Street. Embrace
parents, siblings, nieces and nephews,
kiss friends on cheeks, shake hands with new

acquaintances, drape arms around
friends' shoulders, sing and dance in pubs
on joyful Doolin winter nights.

Run the green shores of Galway Bay
through morning mist and fog. Scale Scafell
Pike, rest at the summit, gaze upon

Derwent Water, Helvellyn, Bowfell,
Windermere, Yewbarrow and Skiddaw.
Surf at Torquay. Barrack at the 'G

with mates eating pies, drinking VB.
Drive from Melbourne to Willunga,
visit ancestors' graves at Saint

Joseph's. Spend hours in snugs with friends
drinking porter and whiskey, discuss
poetry and music, learn inner lives.

Sip limoncello on the Amalfi
coast as the sun sets over the sapphire
waters of the Fiordo di Furore.

Homescape

For Tricia; after Annemarie Ní Churreáin's Florida Wedding

As a twentieth anniversary
gift, I give you the East Beach,

a seven-kilometre curve
of sand, dunes, seaweed, shells

and dune-grass from the Griffiths
Island lighthouse to the golf club.

I give you entry to the waters
of the Southern Ocean, fresh

from Bass Strait. I give you sets
of crystal rolling in from the east,

arriving home on the seaweed-
strewn sand. I give you the Norfolk

Island pines and their shade, refuge
from January sun. I give you

childhood sandcastles, surfing
lessons, near-drownings, the Battery

Hill cannon, Cornettos
from the kiosk at the Surf

Lifesaving Club, warm showers
in the public toilets, steaming

fish and chips in the carpark,
yellow and red flags, Pac-Man

in the café on Sackville Street,
dolphins and seals in the Moyne.

I give you the Southern Ocean
in every season, from winter

storms to spring tides. I give
you the landscape of home,

where you will scatter my ashes.

Notes

"Freight Train:" the line "I can always hear a freight train" is from the Counting Crows song "Raining in Baltimore" from the album *August and Everything After* (Geffen, 1993).

"February:" the line "February, month of despair" is from Margaret Atwood's poem "February" from *Morning in the Burned House* (Houghton Mifflin, 1995).

"Virus as Metaphor:" all text taken from the homepage of the *New York Times* online edition on March 28th, 2020.

"The Suburb of the Future:" the poem mimics the rhetoric of the advertising material for the Walsh Ranch residential development in Parker County, Texas.

"Rainwater:" the poem owes a debt to William Carlos Williams' "The Red Wheelbarrow."

"Protection/Prevention:" all text found on the campus of The University of Texas at Arlington during the COVID-19 pandemic.

"Good Friday, 1930:" on April 30, 1930, at 8:45pm, the BBC announced, "There is no news." The poem was commissioned for the anthology *No News: 90 Poets Reflect on a Unique BBC Newscast,* ed. Paul Munden, Alvin Pang and Shane Strange, Recent Work Press, 2020.

"Warhol:" the poem responds to Andy Warhol's "Self-Portrait" (1986) in the Modern Art Museum of Fort Worth.

"Sweet Movement:" this poem utilizes the terminal form (purportedly invented by the Australian poet John Tranter), incorporating the final word from each line of George and Ira Gershwin's song "Embraceable You," specifically the version performed by Ella Fitzgerald. Additionally, the poem uses the same number of lines, syllables per line, and stanza/verse/chorus structure as Fitzgerald's version of the song. The poem was commissioned by the EastSide Arts Festival 2020, Belfast, Northern Ireland.

"July Evening:" the poem responds to Patrick Kavanagh's poem "Inniskeen Road: July Evening."

"Confession:" the phrase "get me a little oblivion" is from the Counting Crows song "Perfect Blue Buildings" from the album *August and Everything After* (Geffen, 1993).

"Florentine Discourse:" a found poem. All words in the poem were overheard in Florence, Italy.

"Homesickness (Remix):" all text taken from *The Irish Times*, January 25, 2020.

Author Biography

Irish-Australian poet Nathanael O'Reilly teaches creative writing at The University of Texas at Arlington. His ten previous collections include *Selected Poems of Ned Kelly* (Beir Bua Press, 2023), *Dear Nostalgia* (above/ground press, 2023), *Boulevard* (Beir Bua Press, 2021), *(Un)belonging* (Recent Work Press, 2020), *BLUE* (above/ground press, 2020), *Preparations for Departure* (University of Western Australia Publishing, 2017) and *Distance* (Ginninderra Press, 2015). His poetry appears in over one hundred journals and anthologies published in fourteen countries, including *Another Chicago Magazine, Anthropocene, Cordite Poetry Review, The Elevation Review, New World Writing Quarterly, Mascara Literary Review, Trasna, Westerly* and *Wisconsin Review*. He is the poetry editor for *Antipodes: A Global Journal of Australian/New Zealand Literature*.

www.ingramcontent.com/pod-product-compliance
Lightning Source LLC
Chambersburg PA
CBHW031407160426
43196CB00007B/927